Wise Ways

By

Andrea Hughes

This book is dedicated to all my beautiful and sweet grand-children that I love very much Amelia, Wesley, River, Hayden, Jack, Luke, Margot, SJ, Diem, Marlee, Bella, Kaya, Sander Eleanor, Noah and Brighton

Wise Ways

It all began on a hike in the mountains with the 4-H group. The kids were talking as they walked along the dirt road. Though it was late June, it was spring in the mountains and the leaves on the trees shown a bright green. Wild flowers dotted the hillside like an artists palette and chipmunks and squirrels chatted happily in the tall pines.

River ran and climbed up on a big rock inhaling deeply.

"Isn't it beautiful up here, the air is so fresh and clean. I wish it could be like this down in the city." He jumped off the rock and started walking along with Amelia.

"Did you guys see the six o'clock news last night? There was another gang related robbery in our neighborhood. This world is getting to be a scary place with all the violence and crime everywhere." Bella, taller than all the others with long blond hair almost to her waist was thoughtful and serious.

"Not to mention all the pollution everywhere. It is nice to be here in the mountains where we can breathe some fresh air." Ellie who was energetic and petite, took a deep breath too.

"Jack who was known to be the studious one at school chimed in. I wonder what it's going to be like in another fifty years? People won't even be able to come out of their houses without wearing gas masks because the pollution is getting so bad"

"Yeah, maybe the whole world will become extinct unless some changes are made and fast!" SJ picked up a rock and threw it as far and fast as he could down the road. S J was athletic and had a blond shock of hair he wore standing straight up because of all the mousse he put on it.

River chimed in. "I wonder why there is always a war going on somewhere in the world?"

Bella answered, " I don't know. Wouldn't it be great if everyone in the world could live in peace?"

"Yeah and there wasn't any poverty," Ellie added.

Amelia had been quiet until now, "And no problems with homelessness or gangs."

"We need some help!"SJ added.

"What we need is some hope!" said Diem

"What we need is some healing!" added Bella

"What we need is some harmony!" chimed in Amelia

Suddenly they heard a beautiful sound coming from the forest it sounded like the echo of a harp with bird song as accompaniment.

Help, Hope, Healing, and Harmony

Help, Hope, Healing, and Harmony

That's how it has to be

So we can all be free

Healing and Harmony

Helping our Families

The melody had a mystical and beautiful sound like nothing the children had ever heard before. A mist started coming through the trees in the forest along the side of the road and then a tall wizard in dark blue robes that shimmered through the trees appeared to the children. He spoke in a mysterious voice that sounded like the wind.

"You are looking for some help? Your are looking for some hope? Your are looking for some healing? You are looking for some harmony? To find all of these things you must first look in the mirror. To heal the earth must begin with you. You must love and heal yourself. You are very important and can make a big difference, more than you may realize. As you look in the mirror at yourself, you will find many secrets that will help you heal yourself and the world around you. But you must be very still and listen. Keep your senses and heart open and wise teachers will give you the secrets. Now go each of you, in a different direction to somewhere in the world you love. There, you will find the secrets to healing yourself and in turn the world around you." Then the wizard vanished into the mist as quickly as he had appeared. The kids looked at each other in awe and confusion.

"Did that just happen?" Amelia looked at the others with huge blue eyes.

"I saw him too," said River

"What do you make of what he told us?" said Bella

"Let's sit down and talk about it," Jack said.

The children went over to a grassy area at the side of the road and sat down.

Jack started the conversation, "Well, it's probably a good idea to take heed to what the wizard said."

"Yeah, I agree, What is it about the world that you love the most?" Ellie asked the group.

"My favorite place is the desert and the Red-rock country. We go there every year to see all the cool rock formations. I'm going to go there next week," said River.

The beach and lying out in the sun is my favorite place. We're going on vacation in a month or so. I can't wait! The sun is my favorite thing about the earth piped in SJ.

"I agree that the beach is great but that's because the ocean is there. My favorite thing on earth is water. I love all kinds of water, lakes, rivers, waterfalls, springs. But my favorite of all is the ocean. We're planning a vacation to the Oregon coast. I can't wait to see the ocean again," said Bella.

A little chipmunk ran up on a rock near them.

"Look at that little chipmunk. Isn't he cute? "My favorite thing about the earth is animals. Animals are so cool. Each one is different and unique and adds something to our world. I'm going to go spend some time with my favorite animals, my cat and my horse," said Amelia.

"I love animals too," said Ellie. The earth just wouldn't be the same without them. One reason I love the woods and the forests is because you can find so many animals living freely and happily without their habitats being taken over by people over developing and over populating the earth. There are also all the beautiful flowers, and butterflies. I'm going to go exploring in the woods. That's my favorite thing!"

"Rainbows are my favorite thing in the whole wide world! They are just so magical!" said Diem.

"I just love studying the sky and the stars with my telescope. I am going to look into space. That's what really sparks my imagination!" said Jack.

After the hike all the children began to pay attention to the things they loved about the earth and what the wizard had told them.

One day SJ woke up and it was a beautiful day and the sun was shining brightly. He walked outside and heard the birds singing.

Well, everybody has gone off to find their own secret he thought, but it's a beautiful day and the sun feels so good. I think I'll just lay down here in the sun and catch a few rays. He felt the warm sun shining down on him and then he heard a deep but warm voice echo in his ears.

"I am Grandfather Sun. You can learn much about healing the earth from me. Share your own light with others as I share my light with everyone on earth. Share your energy to make the world a better place as I share my energy with you. Let your light shine, like the sun shines."

Then a beautiful melody surrounded SJ

Let your light shine like the sun shines

Send out some golden rays

Let your light shine like the sun shines

Change the night to day

Let your light shine like the sun shines

Wherever you may go

Let your light shine like the sun shines

Give your smile a happy glow

Let your light shine, like the sun shines

Share your energy

Let your light shine, like the sun shines

Help the world be free

Let your light shine like the sun shines

Lift up and help your friends

Let your light shine like the sun shines

And the love will never end

"Thank you Grandfather Sun. I'll remember to let my light shine like you let your light shine on me and everyone else on the earth!"

Meanwhile Bella was vacationing with her family in Oregon by the ocean. The Ocean is so beautiful and peaceful she thought. I love watching the tides roll in and out. I always feel so calm listening to the waves crash and watching the gulls fly. I wish I could stay longer but it's getting dark. Look at that beautiful moon rising over the water.

Suddenly she heard a beautiful mystical melody and a mist appeared and then a figure in the mist.

"I am Grandmother Moon and I watch over all the waters, oceans and tides, as well all the finned ones that use me as their home. I am hear to teach you to flow like water flows. Life is always changing. Learn to go with the flow of changes and make changes that need to be made to improve the earth. Water always recycles. Learn to be like water and recycle whatever and whenever you can. Remember, go with the flow."

Flow like the ocean, Flow like the sea

Go with the motion, feel ever free

Go with the changes that life always brings

Life rearranges the song that it sings

Flow like the ocean, flow like the sea

You might have a notion how free you can be

Go with the flowing, the cycles of life

Soon you'll be knowing there's no need for strife

Bella said, "Thank you Grandmother moon. I'll remember that life is always changing and that I can make changes too that need to be made. I will remember to go with the flow!"

Jack had just hiked up to the top of a mountain to set up his telescope.

"That was quite a hike but worth it!. Look at the view up here and the air is so pure and clean. Blue sky is everywhere! Now I just need to wait until it gets dark to see all the stars in space. Wow! Look at that eagle! I wish I could fly and soar like he does."

Then Jack heard a low and deep voice and saw a vision in the sky.

"I am Father Sky. I look after the clouds and the weather as well as all the winged ones that love to fly through me. I also give you all the fresh air you breathe. I am in charge of all the brother's and sister's in the great star nation. All the stars, moons, suns, and planets spin through me. I want you to remember to keep your sights and goals high. Don't be afraid to go for your dreams. Keep your thoughts pure like my air is pure here at the top of the mountains.

Don't forget to fly high in the sky and spread out your wings. Then a beautiful melody flowed through the sky."

Fly high in the sky, spread out your wings

Fly high in the sky, hold on to your dreams

Fly through the air, learn to be free

Do what you dare, see what you can see

Fly high in the sky, just like a bird

Keep your goals high, be true to your world

See how far you can go to reach for the stars

Then you will know the strength of your powers.

Fly High

"Thank you Father Sky"said Jack. I'll try to be brave and true to what I believe and keep my thoughts pure as clean air. I will keep my goals high to reach for those stars!"

Ellie found her favorite woods to explore. "I just love walking in the woods. Trees are so beautiful. Trees are the kindest thing I know. They just provide nice cool shade and grow. Native Americans call them The Standing People. I like thinking of them as people. Look at all the wild flowers growing and that big butterfly. I have never seen something that spectacular in my life!" The Butterfly started getting bigger and bigger until it was as big as a person.

"Hello, I am the Butterfly Fairy. I represent everything beautiful and precious about the earth. I watch over all the breathtaking beauty you see like flowers, waterfalls, sunsets, and all the beauty in nature. I am hear to tell you to always look for and appreciate all the beauty in this world and enjoy being out in nature. Nature and it's beauty can always be a healing tool. Remember look for the good and the beautiful." And then the Butterfly Fairy started singing.

Look for the good and the beautiful, instead of the dreary and sad

Look for the joy and the miracle, That way your heart can be glad

Look for the wise and the wonderful, Nurture nature wherever you go

Notice the beauty that's everywhere, Bask in the Sun's setting glow

Look for the good and the beautiful, Your heart will be glad if you do

Enjoy all the beauty that life can bring,

 And you will know peace through and through

"Thank you Butterfly Fairy. You're right. It is such a beautiful world. I need to remember that when I get discouraged about life sometimes."

"You are the cutest, sweetest kitty. You are the cuddliest kitty in the whole wide world! I love you so much!"said Amelia. "I can't decide if I love you or my horse Goldi more. Animals are just the best thing in the whole wide world! I just love all the animals!"

A voice came out of nowhere it seemed and then a magical woman appeared in front of Amelia.

"Hello, I am the Animal Friend. We love the two-leggeds too but sometimes we feel that they have forgotten us and and the places we need to live. They keep taking away our swamps and our forests and building on every piece of land. I am here to help you to remember to leave some room for the wild things and the places they live. We are all a family of living creatures on the earth and it is important to share our habitats." Then a drum began to sound and she began this chant.

The bear is our brother, we must take care of him

The bear is our brother, we must take care of him

The winged ones are our sisters, we must take care of them,

The winged ones are our sisters, we must take care of them

The wolf is are our brother, we must take care of him,

The wolf is our brother, we must take care of him

The deer are our sisters, we must take care of them

The deer are our sisters, we must take care of them

The whales are our brothers, we must take care of them,

The whales are our brothers, we must take care of them

The Earth is our mother, we must take care of her,

The Earth is our mother, we must take Care of her

"Thank You Animal Friend," said Amelia, "We must treat all of our animal friends as if they are our brothers and sisters in the great earth family."

It had just finished raining and the sun was peaking through the clouds when Diem spotted a beautiful rainbow and gave out a squeal. She ran outside to get a better look at it.

"I finally found a rainbow which is my favorite thing in the whole world. Rainbows are so magical but they are kind of hard to find when you want to find one. They can be a happy surprise when they appear. But isn't it lovely! You can see every color."

There was a symphony of sound and then a beautiful Rainbow Princess appeared.

"I am the Rainbow Princess and I create all the beautiful colors you see everywhere and all the magic of rainbows. I am here to teach you to appreciate each and every color of the rainbow and each and every person on the earth no matter what their hair or skin color is because everyone is beautiful just the way they are. Just like the colors in a rainbow work in harmony to make it beautiful, so every person on earth should work together in harmony to make the world a better place. You mustn't separate in to little groups but always work together throughout the world and appreciate each other's strengths and differences. Everyone can make an important contribution to our world. Remember to all work together in harmony."

Then she began to sing a beautiful melodious tune

We need all the colors of the rainbow to show us the beauty in our world

We need all the colors of the people to show us the beauty in our world

Every color has the perfect light, the perfect color that can make the rainbow bright

Every person has a special song, their own music they can bring along

We need all the colors of the rainbow ,to share their own special ray

We need all the colors of the people, so all can join in and say

That every color can join in to sing about the beauty every color brings

We need all the colors of the rainbow to show us the beauty in our world

We need all the colors of the people to show us the beauty in our world

"Thank you Rainbow Princess, I will remember to appreciate every color of the rainbow and every person in the world." Then the Rainbow Princess vanished and the rainbow began to fade away.

River was walking through the beautiful red rock formations with his family.

"Look at the rock formations here. Mother nature is such a wonderful sculptor and artist. Some of these rocks almost look like they could come alive and become giant creatures!" He wandered over to study a sandstone arch and as he looked through it, a mystical vision came to him through the arch.

"I am Mother Earth and I watch over everything on the earth. I watch over all the winged ones that fly through the air and all the finned ones that swim in the waters, all the mountains and valleys. I watch over everything that lives on this planet and even the non-living things like stone people and the beautiful rock formations on the earth. I am even in charge of volcanos and new land forming on the earth. I give much love and life to the earth but my heart is aching because many have not returned that love and have not taken care of your Mother Earth. Remember everyone must have a heart and do your part to love your Mother and take care of her." Then she began singing a lovely song that sounded like a lullabye.

Have a heart and do your part, with yourself is where it starts

Don't forget your destiny, You're the one that has the key

Have a heart and do your part, make good choices, that's a start

If you do your life will be, a happier one, just try and see

Have a heart, do your part, Look for good things, that's a start

Believe in good things everywhere, Do what you can to show you care

Have a heart, Do your part, Share the wealth is where it starts

Give what you can to help someone, That way there is twice the fun

Have a heart, Do your part, Be glad you're different, that's a start

Just think how boring things would be if you all looked the same as me

Have a heart, do your part to heal our world is where it starts

We all must help in everyway, to make things better every day

So have a heart, have a heart, everyone must have a heart

Do your part to help and heal, you'll be surprised how good you feel

"You're right Mother Earth! What would we ever do without you. We wouldn't be alive! We must all do our part to take care of and love our Mother Earth!

One day all the friends on that hike got together and shared what they had learned when they visited the things they loved most in the world. They shared their important lessons with each other and then they started to sing the song that the Wizard had sung to them together.

Help, Hope, Healing, and Harmony

That's how it has to be

So we can all be free

Healing and Harmony

Helping our Families

Help, Hope, Healing and Harmony

Teach others how to see

That's how it has to be

Healing and Harmony

Helping our Families

The End

More Books By This Author:

Horses for the Heart

Cat Tales

The Rainbow World

Re-Enchanting the Forest

Creatures in the Garden